OSCARIANA ✎

THE WIT & MAXIMS OF OSCAR WILDE

OSCARIANA ✿

THE WIT & MAXIMS OF OSCAR WILDE

COLLECTED BY
STEPHEN CALLOWAY & DAVID COLVIN

LONDON : MIIIM

ORION
MEDIA

FIRST PUBLISHED IN 1997 BY
ORION MEDIA
AN IMPRINT OF ORION BOOKS LTD
ORION HOUSE
5 UPPER ST. MARTIN'S LANE, LONDON WC2H 9EA
COPYRIGHT © ORION BOOKS LTD

DESIGNED AT THE CYPHER

A CIP CATALOGUE RECORD FOR THIS BOOK
IS AVAILABLE FROM THE BRITISH LIBRARY

ISBN 0752 81 040 5

PRINTED AND BOUND IN GREAT BRITAIN
BY RICHARD CLAYS LTD, ST IVES PLC

I WAS A MAN WHO STOOD IN SYMBOLIC relations to the art and culture of my age. I realised this for myself at the very dawn of my manhood, and forced my age to realise it afterwards. Few men hold such a position in their lifetime and have it so acknowledged. It is usually discerned, if it is discerned at all, by the historian, or the critic, long after both the man and his age have passed away. With me it was different. I felt it myself, and made others feel it.

I made art a philosophy, and philosophy an art : I altered the minds of men, and the colour of things : I awoke the imagination of my century so that it created myth and legend around me : I summed up all things in a phrase, all existence in an epigram : whatever I touched I made beautiful.

From DE PROFUNDIS

PHRASES
AND PHILOSOPHIES
FOR THE USE OF THE YOUNG

❦

T HE FIRST DUTY in life is to be as artificial as possible. What the second duty is no one has as yet discovered.

Wickedness is a myth invented by good people to account for the curious attractiveness of others.

If the poor only had profiles there would be no difficulty in solving the problem of poverty.

Those who see any difference between soul and body have neither.

A really well-made buttonhole is the only link between Art and Nature.

Religions die when they are proved to be true. Science is the record of dead religions.

The well-bred contradict other people. The wise contradict themselves.

Nothing that actually occurs is of the smallest importance.

Dullness is the coming of age of seriousness.

In all unimportant matters, style, not sincerity, is the essential. In all important matters, style, not sincerity, is the essential.

If one tells the truth, one is sure, sooner or later, to be found out.

Pleasure is the only thing one should live for. Nothing ages like happiness.

It is only by not paying one's bills that one can hope to live in the memory of the commercial classes.

No crime is vulgar, but all vulgarity is crime. Vulgarity is the conduct of others.

Only the shallow know themselves.

Time is waste of money.

One should always be a little improbable.

There is a fatality about all good resolutions. They are invariably made too soon.

The only way to atone for being occasionally a little over-dressed is by being always absolutely over-educated.

To be premature is to be perfect.

Any preoccupation with ideas of what is right or wrong in conduct shows an arrested intellectual development.

Ambition is the last refuge of the failure.

A truth ceases to be true when more than one person believes in it.

In examinations the foolish ask questions that the wise cannot answer.

Greek dress was in its essence inartistic. Nothing should reveal the body but the body.

One should either be a work of art, or wear a work of art.

It is only the superficial qualities that last. Man's deeper nature is soon found out.

Industry is the root of all ugliness.

The ages live in history through their anachronisms.

It is only the gods who taste of death. Apollo has passed away, but Hyacinth, whom men say he slew, lives on. Nero and Narcissus are always with us.

The old believe everything : the middle-aged suspect everything : the young know everything.

The condition of perfection is idleness : the aim of perfection is youth.

Only the great masters of style ever succeed in being obscure.

There is something tragic about the enormous number of young men there are in England at the present moment who start life with perfect profiles, and end by adopting some useful profession.

To love oneself is the beginning of a life-long romance.

THE IMPORTANCE
OF BEING EARNEST

MEN OF THE noblest possible
moral character are extremely sus-
ceptible to the influence of the physical
charms of others. Modern, no less than ancient, history supplies us with many most
painful examples of what I refer to. If it
were not so, indeed, history would be quite
unreadable.

The only way to behave to a woman is to
make love to her, if she is pretty, and to some
one else if she is plain.

Relations are simply a tedious pack
of people who haven't got the remotest
knowledge of how to live nor the smallest instinct about when to die.

Nothing annoys people so much as not
receiving invitations.

I am not in favour of long engagements. They give people the opportunity of finding out each others character before marriage, which I think is never advisable.

One should never trust a woman who tells one her real age. A woman who would tell one that would tell one anything.

I do not approve of anything that tampers with natural ignorance. Ignorance is like a delicate exotic fruit : touch it, and the bloom is gone. The whole theory of modern education is radically unsound. Fortunately, in England at any rate, education produces no effect whatsoever. If it did it would prove a serious danger to the upper classes, and probably lead to acts of violence in Grosvenor Square.

More than half of modern culture depends on what one shouldn't read.

Girls never marry the men they flirt with. Girls don't think it right. It accounts for the extraordinary number of bachelors that one sees all over the place.

When one is placed in the position of guardian one has to adopt a very high moral tone on all subjects. It's one's duty to do so. But a high moral tone can hardly be said to conduce very much to either one's health or one's happiness.

I do not approve of the modern sympathy with invalids. I consider it morbid. Illness of any kind is hardly a thing to be encouraged in others. Health is the primary duty of life.

My own business always bores me to death. I prefer other people's.

When I am in trouble eating is the only thing that consoles me. Indeed, when I am in really great trouble, as anyone who knows me intimately will tell you, I refuse everything except food and drink.

When one is going to lead an entirely new life one requires regular and wholesome meals.

By persistently remaining single a man converts himself into a permanent public temptation. Men should be more careful ; this very celibacy leads weaker vessels astray.

No woman should be ever quite accurate about her age. It looks so calculating.

Everybody is clever now-a-days. You can't go anywhere without meeting clever people. This has become an absolute public nuisance.

It is a terrible thing for a man to find out suddenly that all his life he has been speaking nothing but the truth.

Never speak disrespectfully of society. Only people who can't get into it do that.

Thirty-five is a very attractive age. London society is full of women who have of their own free choice remained thirty-five for years.

It is always painful to part with people whom one has known for a very brief space of time. The absence of old friends one can endure with equanimity. But even a momentary separation from anyone to whom one has just been introduced is almost unbearable.

Once a man begins to neglect his domestic duties he becomes painfully effeminate, does he not? And I don't like that. It makes men so very attractive.

In matters of grave importance, style, not sincerity, is the vital thing.

It is very vulgar to talk about one's business. Only people like stockbrokers do that, and then merely at dinner-parties.

In married life three is company and two is none.

It is awfully hard work doing nothing. However, I don't mind hard work when there is no definite object of any kind.

It is very painful for me to be forced to speak the truth. It is the first time in my life that I have ever been reduced to such a painful position, and I am really quite inexperienced in doing anything of the kind.

Few parents now-a-days pay any regard

to what their children say to them. The old-fashioned respect for the young is fast dying out.

If the lower orders don't set us a good example what on earth is the use of them ? They seem, as a class, to have absolutely no sense of moral responsibility.

When one is in town one amuses oneself. When one is in the country one amuses other people. It is excessively boring.

I really don't see anything romantic about proposing. It is very romantic to be in love, but there is nothing romantic about a definite proposal. Why, one may be accepted. One usually is, I believe. Then the excitement is all over. The very essence of romance is uncertainty.

The truth isn't quite the sort of thing that one tells to a nice, sweet, refined girl.

If one plays good music people don't listen, and if one plays bad music people don't talk.

What between the duties expected of

one during one's lifetime and the duties ex-
acted from one after one's death land has
ceased to be either a profit or a pleasure. It
gives one position and prevents one from
keeping it up.

The truth is rarely pure and never simple. Modern life would be very tedious if it
were either, and modern literature a complete impossibility.

The number of women in London who
flirt with their own husbands is perfectly
scandalous. It looks so bad. It is simply
washing one's clean linen in public.

All women become like their mothers
—that is their tragedy. No man does. That
is his.

I don't play accurately—anyone can play
accurately—but I play with wonderful
expression. As far as the piano is concerned sentiment is my forte. I keep science
for life.

I pity any woman who is married to a
man called John. She would probably nev-

er be allowed to know the entrancing pleasure of a single moment's solitude.

To be born, or at any rate bred, in a
handbag, whether it had handles or not,
seems to me to display a contempt for the
ordinary decencies of family life that re-
minds one of the worst excesses of the
French Revolution.

AN IDEAL HUSBAND

❦

LIFE is never fair. And perhaps it is a good thing for most of us that it is not.

Secrets from other people's wives are a necessary luxury in modern life. So, at least, I am told at the club by people who are bald enough to know. But no man should have a secret from his own wife. She invariably finds it out. Women have a wonderful instinct about things. They discover everything except the obvious.

Optimism begins in a broad grin, and Pessimism ends with blue spectacles. They are both of them merely poses.

The strength of women comes from the fact that psychology cannot explain us. Men can be analysed, women—merely adored.

There is some flaw in each one of us.

In old days nobody pretended to be a bit better than his neighbour. In fact, to be a bit better than one's neighbour was considered excessively vulgar and middle class. Now-a-days, with our modern mania for morality, everyone has to pose as a paragon of purity, incorruptibility, and all the other seven deadly virtues. And what is the result ? We all go over like ninepins—one after the other.

Morality is simply the attitude we adopt towards people whom we personally dislike.

A woman who can keep a man's love, and love him in return, has done all the world wants of women, or should want of them.

If there were less sympathy in the world there would be less trouble in the world.

Women who have common sense are so curiously plain.

There is only one tragedy in a woman's life—the fact that her past is always her lover, and her future invariably her husband.

If we men married the women we deserved, we should have a very bad time of it.

How many men there are in modern life who would like to see their past burning to white ashes before them.

Loveless marriages are horrible. But there is one thing worse than an absolutely loveless marriage—a marriage in which there is love, but on one side only.

Questions are never indiscreet; answers sometimes are.

Public and private life are different things. They have different laws and move on different lines.

Men can love what is beneath them— things unworthy, stained, dishonoured. We women worship when we love; and when we lose our worship we lose everything.

An acquaintance that begins with a compliment is sure to develop into a real friendship. It starts in the right manner.

Women are never disarmed by compliments. Men always are. That is the difference between the two sexes.

One's past is what one is. It is the only way by which people should be judged.

I am always saying what I shouldn't say ; in fact, I usually say what I really think—a great mistake nowadays. It makes one so liable to be misunderstood.

There are terrible temptations that it requires strength—strength and courage—to yield to. To stake all one's life on one throw —whether the stake be for power or pleasure I care not—there is no weakness in that. There is a horrible, a terrible, courage.

It is always worth while asking a question, though it is not always worth while answering one.

Musical people are so absurdly unreasonable. They always want one to be perfectly dumb at the very moment when one is longing to be absolutely deaf.

Nothing is so dangerous as being too

modern. One is apt to grow old-fashioned quite suddenly.

I think that in practical life there is something about success, actual success, that is a little unscrupulous, something about ambition that is unscrupulous always. Once a man has set his heart and soul on getting to a certain point, if he has to climb the crag, he climbs the crag ; if he has to walk in the mire, he walks in the mire.

Every man of ambition has to fight his century with its own weapons. What this century worships is wealth. The god of this century is wealth. To succeed one must have wealth. At all costs one must have wealth.

The English can't stand a man who is always saying he is in the right, but they are very fond of a man who admits he has been in the wrong. It is one of the best things in them.

I don't think man has much capacity for development. He has got as far as he can, and that is not far, is it ?

It is not the perfect but the imperfect who have need of love. It is when we are wounded by our own hands, or by the hands of others, that love should come to cure us—else what use is love at all.

I am not quite sure that I quite know what pessimism really means. All I do know is that life cannot be understood without much charity, cannot be lived without much charity. It is love that is the explanation of this world, whatever may be the explanation of the next.

There is more to be said for stupidity than people imagine. Personally, I have a great admiration for stupidity. It is a sort of fellow-feeling, I suppose.

In England people actually try to be brilliant at breakfast. That is so dreadful of them. Only dull people are brilliant at breakfast.

Our husbands never appreciate anything in us. We have to go to others for that.

I wouldn't marry a man with a future before him for anything under the sun.

I never knew what terror was before ; I know it now. It is as if a hand of ice were laid upon one's heart. It is as if one's heart were beating itself to death in some empty hollow.

She wore far too much rouge last night and not quite enough clothes. That is always a sign of despair in a woman.

Mrs. Cheveley is one of those very modern women of our time who find a new scandal as becoming as a new bonnet, and air them both in the Park every afternoon at 5.30. I am sure she adores her own scandals, and that the sorrow of her life at present is that she can't manage to have enough of them.

A WOMAN
OF NO IMPORTANCE

❦

Y OU CAN'T make people good by
Act of Parliament—that is something.

When one is in love one begins by deceiving oneself, and one ends by deceiving
others. That is what the world calls a romance.

English women conceal their feelings till
after they are married. They show them then.

Nothing should be out of reach of hope.
Life is hope.

One should sympathise with the joy, the
beauty, the colour of life. The less said a-
bout life's sores the better.

Nothing is so aggravating as calmness.
There is something positively brutal about

the good temper of most modern men. I wonder we women stand it as well as we do.

I don't believe in the existence of Puritan women. I don't think there is a woman in the world who would not be a little flattered if one made love to her. It is that which makes women so irresistibly adorable.

The soul is is born old, but grows young. That is the comedy of life. The body is born young, and grows old. That is life's tragedy.

One can survive everything now-a-days except death, and live down anything except a good reputation.

Intellectual generalities are always interesting, but generalities in morals mean absolutely nothing.

To be in society is merely a bore, but to be out of it simply a tragedy.

One can always know at once whether a man has home claims upon his life or not. I have noticed a very, very sad expression in the eyes of so many married men.

A bad man is the sort of a man who admires innocence. A bad woman is the sort of a woman a man never gets tired of.

The only difference between the saint and the sinner is that every saint has a past, and every sinner has a future.

To get into the best society now-a-days one has either to feed people, amuse people, or shock people—that is all.

Duty is what one expects from others, it is not what one does one's self.

A really grande passion is comparatively rare now-a-days. It is the privilege of people who have nothing to do. That is the one use of the idle classes.

There is no secret of life. Life's aim, if it has one, is simply to be always looking for temptations. There are not nearly enough of them ; I sometimes pass a whole day without coming across a single one. It is quite dreadful. It makes one so nervous about the future.

The secret of life is never to have an emotion that is unbecoming.

All thought is immoral. Its very essence is destruction. If you think of anything you kill it ; nothing survives being thought of.

No woman should have a memory. Memory in a woman is the beginning of dowdiness. One can always tell from a woman's bonnet whether she has got a memory or not.

There are things that are right to say, but that may be said at the wrong time and to the wrong people.

To elope is cowardly ; it is running away from danger, and danger has become so rare in modern life.

When a man is old enough to do wrong he should be old enough to do right also.

The Book of Life begins with a man and a woman in a garden. It ends with Revelations.

All men are married women's property.

That is the only true definition of what married women's property really is.

Talk to every woman as if you loved her and to every man as if he bored you, and at the end of your first season you will have the reputation of possessing the most perfect social tact.

Man—poor, awkward, reliable, necessary man—belongs to a sex that has been rational for millions and millions of years. He can't help himself ; it is in his race. The history of women is very different. They have always been picturesque protests against the mere existence of common-sense ; they saw its dangers from the first.

Discontent is the first step in the progress of a man or a nation.

More marriages are ruined now-a-days by the common-sense of the husband than by anything else. How can a woman be expected to be happy with a man who insists on treating her as if she were a perfectly rational being.

I adore simple pleasures. They are the last refuge of the complex.

Men always want to be a woman's first love. That is their clumsy vanity. Women have a more subtle instinct about things. What they like is to be a man's last romance.

A man who can dominate a London dinner table can dominate the world. The future belongs to the dandy. It is the exquisites who are going to rule.

Men marry because they are tired, women because they are curious. Both are disappointed.

Women are a fascinatingly wilful sex. Every woman is a rebel, and usually in wild revolt against herself.

One should always be in love. That is the reason one should never marry.

The history of women is the history of the worst form of tyranny the world has ever known : the tyranny of the weak over the strong. It is the only tyranny that lasts.

The happiness of a married man depends on the people he has not married.

The world has been made by fools that wise men may live in it.

Women love us for our defects. If we have enough of them they will forgive us everything.

Society is a necessary thing. No man has any real success in this world unless he has got women to back him—and women rule society. If you have not got women on your side you are quite over. You might just as well be a barrister or a stockbroker or a journalist at once.

He must be quite respectable. One has never heard his name before in the whole course of one's life, which speaks volumes for a man now-a-days.

The Peerage is the one book a young man about town should know thoroughly, and it is the best thing in fiction the English have ever done.

The world has always laughed at its own

tragedies, that being the only way in which it has been able to bear them. Consequently whatever the world has treated seriously belongs to the comedic side of things.

You should never try to understand women. Women are pictures, men are problems. If you want to know what a woman really means—which, by the way, is always a dangerous thing to do—look at her, don't listen to her.

To have been well brought up is a great drawback now-a-days. It shuts one out from so much.

Nothing refines but the intellect.

Twenty years of romance make a woman look like a ruin ; but twenty years of marriage make her something like a public building.

Men know life too early ; women know life too late—that is the difference between men and women.

I delight in men over seventy. They always offer one the devotion of a lifetime.

I feel sure that if I lived in the country for six months I should become so unsophisticated that no one would take the slightest notice of me.

One should never take sides in anything. Taking sides is the beginning of sincerity, and earnestness follows shortly afterwards, and the human being becomes a bore.

Plain women are always jealous of their husbands; beautiful women never are. They never have time. They are always so occupied in being jealous of other people's husbands.

I adore London dinner parties. The clever people never listen and the stupid people never talk.

One knows so well the popular idea of health. The English country gentleman galloping along after a fox—the unspeakable in pursuit of the uneatable.

LADY WINDERMERE'S FAN

❧

LONDON is too full of fogs and serious people. Whether the fogs produce
the serious people or whether the serious
people produce the fogs I don't know.

I don't like compliments : I don't see
why a man should think he is pleasing a
woman enormously when he says to her a
whole heap of things that he doesn't mean.

Now-a-days people seem to look on life
as a speculation. It is not a speculation. It
is a sacrament. Its ideal is love. Its purification is sacrifice.

Because the husband is vile—should the
wife be vile also ?

It is absurd to divide people into good and
bad. People are either charming or tedious.

If a woman wants to hold a man she has merely to appeal to what is worst in him. We make gods of men and they leave us. Others make brutes of them and they fawn and are faithful.

Our husbands would really forget our existence if we didn't nag at them from time to time, just to remind them that we have a perfect legal right to do so.

It is a dangerous thing to reform anyone.

People cannot be divided into the good and the bad, as though they were two separate races or creations. What are called good women may have terrible things in them, mad moods of recklessness, assertion, jealousy, sin. Bad women, as they are termed, may have in them sorrow, repentance, pity, sacrifice.

Men become old, but they never become good.

There are moments when one has to choose between living one's own life, fully, entirely, completely—or dragging out some false, shallow, degrading existence that the world in its hypocrisy demands.

Crying is the refuge of plain women, but the ruin of pretty ones.

It is strange that men who love and who teach their wives to love, should pass from the love that is given to the love that is bought.

London is full of women who trust their husbands. One can always recognise them. They look so thoroughly unhappy.

Between men and women there is no friendship possible. There is passion, enmity, worship, love—but no friendship.

Nothing looks so much like innocence as an indiscretion.

There is a great deal of good in Lord Augustus. Fortunately it is all on the surface. Just where good qualities should be.

When men give up saying what is charming they give up thinking what is charming.

Men are such cowards. They outrage every law of the world, and are afraid of the world's tongue.

One pays for one's sins, and then one pays again, and all one's life one pays. Suffering is an expiation.

Wicked women bother one. Good women bore one. That's the only difference between them.

A cynic is a man who knows the price of everything, and the value of nothing. A sentimentalist is a man who sees an absurd value in everything, and doesn't know the market price of any single thing.

Experience is the name everyone gives to their mistakes.

Love is easily killed.

What a pity that in life we only get our lessons when they are of no use to us.

There is the same world for all of us, and good and evil, sin and innocence, go through it hand in hand. To shut one's eyes to half of life that one may live securely is as though one blinded one's self that one might walk with more safety in a land of pit and precipice.

Misfortunes one can endure, they come from outside, they are accidents. But to suffer for one's faults—ah ! there is the sting of life.

I talk so trivially about life because I think that life is far too important a thing ever to talk seriously about it.

In this world there are only two tragedies. One is not getting what one wants, and the other is getting it. The last is much the worst—the last is a real tragedy.

It takes a thoroughly good woman to do a thoroughly stupid thing.

What is the difference between scandal and gossip ? Oh ! gossip is charming ! History is merely gossip, but scandal is gossip made tedious by morality.

Hopper is one of nature's gentlemen—the worst type of gentleman I know.

All men are monsters. The only thing to do is to feed the wretches well. A good cook does wonders.

A man who moralises is usually a hypocrite, and a woman who moralises is invariably plain. There is nothing in the whole world so unbecoming to a woman as a Nonconformist conscience. And most women know it, I am glad to say.

Women always want one to be good. And if we are good when they meet us, they don't love us at all. They like to find us quite irretrievably bad, and to leave us quite unattractively good.

Experience is a question of instinct about life.

I am afraid that good people do a great deal of harm in this world. Certainly the greatest harm they do is that they make badness of such extraordinary importance.

Now-a-days, to be intelligible is to be found out.

If you pretend to be good the world takes

you very seriously. If you pretend to be bad it doesn't. Such is the astounding stupidity of optimism.

He's sure to be a wonderful success. He thinks like a Tory and talks like a Radical, and that's so important now-a-days.

No nice girl should ever waltz with such particularly younger sons. It looks so fast !

There's nothing in the world like the devotion of a married woman. It's a thing no married man knows anything about.

It's the old, old story. Love—well, not at first sight—but love at the end of the season, which is so much more satisfactory.

How marriage ruins a man. It's as demoralising as cigarettes, and far more expensive.

I won't tell you that the world matters nothing, or the world's voice, or the voice of society. They matter a good deal. They matter far too much.

It is most dangerous now-a-days for a

husband to pay any attention to his wife in public. It always makes people think that he beats her when they're alone. The world has grown so suspicious of anything that looks like a happy married life.

When one has sinned, what consoles one now-a-days is not repentance, but pleasure. Repentance is quite out of date.

I am the only person in the world I should like to know thoroughly, but I don't see any chance of it just at present.

I thought I had no heart. I find I have, and a heart doesn't suit me. Somehow it doesn't go with modern dress. It makes one look old, and it spoils one's career at critical moments.

A mother who doesn't part with a daughter every season has no real affection.

What on earth should we men do going about with purity and innocence ? A carefully thought-out buttonhole is much more effective.

My experience is that as soon as people

are old enough to know better they don't know anything at all.

The world is perfectly packed with good women. To know them is a middle-class education.

We are all in the gutter, but some of us are looking at the stars.

A FEW MAXIMS

❧

E DUCATION is an admirable thing. But it is well to remember from time to time that nothing that is worth knowing can be taught.

Public opinion exists only when there are no ideas.

The English are always degrading truths into facts. When a truth becomes a fact it loses all its intellectual value.

It is a very sad thing that now-a-days there is so little useless information.

The only link between Literature and the Drama left to us in England at the present moment is the bill of the play.

In old days books were written by men of letters and read by the public. Now-a-

days books are written by the public and
read by nobody.

Most women are so artificial that they
have no sense of Art. Most men are so natural that they have no sense of Beauty.

Friendship is far more tragic than love. It
lasts longer.

What is abnormal in Life stands in normal relations to Art. It is the only thing in
Life that stands in normal relations to Art.

A subject that is beautiful in itself gives
no suggestion to the artist. It lacks imperfec-
tion.

The only thing that the artist cannot see
is the obvious. The only thing that the public can see is the obvious. The result is the
criticism of the journalist.

Art is the only serious thing in the world.
And the artist is the only person who is never serious.

To be really mediæval one should have no
body. To be really modern one should have

no soul. To be really Greek one should have no clothes.

Dandyism is the assertion of the absolute modernity of Beauty.

The only thing that can console one for being poor is extravagance. The only thing that can console one for being rich is economy.

One should never listen. To listen is a sign of indifference to one's hearers.

Even the disciple has his uses. He stands behind one's throne, and at the very moment of one's triumph whispers in one's ear that, after all, one is immortal.

The criminal classes are so close to us that even the policeman can see them. They are so far away from us that only the poet can understand them.

Those whom the gods love grow young.

THE PICTURE
OF DORIAN GRAY

THERE IS no such thing as an immoral book. Books are well written, or badly written. That is all.

To influence a person is to give him one's own soul. He does not think his natural thoughts or burn with his natural passions. His virtues are not real to him. His sins, if there are such things as sins, are borrowed. He becomes an echo of someone else's music, an actor of a part that has not been written for him.

There is only one thing in the world worse than being talked about, and that is not being talked about.

The one charm of marriage is that it makes a life of deception necessary for both parties.

Being natural is simply a pose, and the most irritating one I know.

Beauty ends where an intellectual expression begins. Intellect destroys the harmony of any face.

The terror of society, which is the basis of morals, and the terror of God, which is the secret of religion—these are the two things that govern us.

Lady Brandon treats her guests exactly as an auctioneer treats his goods. She either explains them entirely away, or tells one everything about them except what one wants to know.

Conscience and cowardice are really the same things. Conscience is the trade name of the firm.

It is a sad thing to think about, but there is no doubt that Genius lasts longer than Beauty. That accounts for the fact that we all take such pains to over-educate ourselves.

There is nothing that art cannot express.

Poets are not scrupulous. They know how useful passion is for publication. Now-a-days a broken heart will run to many editions.

The worst of having a romance is that it leaves one so unromantic.

One's own soul, and the passions of one's friends—those are the fascinating things of life.

When one is in love, one always begins by deceiving one's self and one always ends by deceiving others. That is what the world calls romance.

I never talk during music—at least good music. If one hears bad music, it is one's duty to drown it by conversation.

Women spoil every romance by trying to make it last forever.

The only artists I have ever known who

are personally delightful are bad artists. Good artists exist simply on what they make, and consequently are perfectly uninteresting in what they are.

A cigarette is the perfect type of a perfect pleasure. It is exquisite, and it leaves one unsatisfied.

There is always something ridiculous about the emotions of people whom one has ceased to love.

There are only two kinds of people who are really fascinating—people who know absolutely everything, and people who know absolutely nothing.

There is a luxury in self-reproach. When we blame ourselves we feel that no one else has a right to blame us. It is the confession, not the priest, that gives us absolution.

Every effect that one produces gives one an enemy. To be popular one must be a mediocrity.

I hate vulgar realism in literature. The

man who could call a spade a spade should be compelled to use one. It is the only thing he is fit for.

There is no such thing as an omen. Destiny does not send us heralds. She is too wise, or too cruel, for that.

Life is not governed by will or intention. Life is a question of the nerves and fibres and slowly built-up cells in which thought hides itself and passion has its dreams.

Man is a being with myriad lives and myriad sensations, a complex, multiform creature that bears within itself strange legacies of thought and passion, and whose very flesh is tainted with the monstrous maladies of the dead.

As long as a woman can look ten years younger than her own daughter she is perfectly satisfied.

There is always something infinitely mean about other people's tragedies.

Shallow sorrows and shallow loves live

on. The loves and sorrows that are great are destroyed by their own plenitude.

Moderation is a fatal thing. Nothing succeeds like excess.

All charming people are spoiled. It is the secret of their attraction.

One's days are too brief to take the burden of another's sorrows on one's shoulders. Each man lives his own life, and pays his own price for living it. The only pity is that one has to pay so often for a single fault. One has to pay over and over again, indeed. In her dealings with man Destiny never closes her accounts.

Pleasure is Nature's test, her sign of approval. When we are happy we are always good, but when we are good we are not always happy.

To reveal art and conceal the artist is art's aim.

The people who love only once in their lives are the really shallow people. What they call their loyalty and their fidelity I call either the lethargy of custom or their lack of imagination.

It is personalities, not principles, that move the age.

To the philosopher women represent the triumph of matter over mind, just as men represent the triumph of mind over morals. The only way a woman can ever reform a man is by boring him so completely that he loses all possible interest in life.

The only horrible thing in the world is ennui. That is the one sin for which there is no forgiveness.

We live in an age when unnecessary things are our only necessities.

I love scandals about other people, but scandals about myself don't interest me. They have not got the charm of novelty.

Moderation is a fatal thing. Enough is as bad as a meal. More than enough is as good as a feast.

One should never make one's début with

a scandal. One should reserve that to give an interest to one's old age.

What man has sought for is, indeed, neither pain nor pleasure, but simply life. Man has sought to live intensely, fully, perfectly. When he can do so without exercising restraint on others, or suffering it ever, when his activities are all pleasurable to him, he will be saner, healthier, more civilised, more himself. When man is happy he is in harmony with himself and his environment.

One can always be kind to people about whom one cares nothing.

I like men who have a future and women who have a past.

Women, as some witty Frenchman put it, inspire us with the desire to do masterpieces, and always prevent us from carrying them out.

Society, civilised society at least, is never very ready to believe anything to the detriment of those who are both rich and fascinating. It instinctively feels that manners are of more importance than morals, and in its opinion the highest respectability is of much less value than the possession of a good chef. And, after all, it is a very poor consolation to be told that the man who has given one a bad dinner or poor wine is irreproachable in his private life. Even the cardinal virtues cannot atone for half-cold entrées.

Punctuality is the thief of time.

Women give to men the very gold of their lives, but they invariably want it back in such very small change.

No artist is ever morbid. The artist can express everything.

Don't tell me that you have exhausted life. When a man says that one knows that life has exhausted him.

When a woman marries again it is because she detested her first husband. When a man marries again it is because he adored his first wife. Women try their luck ; men risk theirs.

Youth ! There is nothing like it. It is

absurd to talk of the ignorance of youth. The only people to whose opinions I listen now with any respect are persons much younger than myself. They seem in front of me. Life has revealed to them her latest wonder.

Romance lives by repetition, and repetition converts an appetite into an art.

All crime is vulgar, just as all vulgarity is crime.

One regrets the loss even of one's worst habits. Perhaps one regrets them the most. They are such an essential part of one's personality.

It often happens that the real tragedies of life occur in such an inartistic manner that they hurt us by their crude violence, their absolute incoherence, their absurd want of meaning, their entire lack of style. They affect us just as vulgarity affects us. They give us an impression of sheer brute force, and we revolt against that.

When a woman finds out that her husband is absolutely indifferent to her, she either becomes dreadfully dowdy or wears very smart bonnets that some other woman's husband has to pay for.

It is a mistake to think that the passion one feels in creation is ever really shown in the work one creates. Art is always more abstract than we fancy. Form and colour tell us of form and colour—that is all.

It is only shallow people who require years to get rid of an emotion. A man who is master of himself can end a sorrow as easily as he can invent a pleasure.

No man ever came across two ideal things. Few come across one.

To become the spectator of one's own life is to escape its suffering.

The worship of the senses has often, and with much justice, been decried, men feeling a natural instinct of terror about passions and sensations that seem stronger than themselves, and which they are conscious of sharing with the less highly-organised forms of existence. But it is probable the true nature of the senses has never been understood, and that they have remained savage and animal merely because the world has sought to starve them into submission or to kill them by pain instead of aiming at making them elements of a new spirituality, of which a fine instinct for beauty will be the dominant characteristic.

Women appreciate cruelty more than anything else. They have wonderfully primitive instincts. We have emancipated them, but they remain slaves, looking for their master all the same. They love being dominated.

Children begin by loving their parents ; as they grow older they judge them. Sometimes they forgive them.

We live in an age that reads too much to be wise, and thinks too much to be beautiful.

You know I am not a champion of marriage. The real drawback to marriage is that it makes one unselfish, and unselfish people are colourless—they lack individuality. Still there are certain temperaments that marriage makes more complex. They retain their egotism, and add to it many other egos. They are forced to have more than one life. They become more highly organised, and to be highly organised is, I should fancy, the object of man's existence. Besides, every experience is of value, and whatever one may say against marriage it is certainly an experience.

Mediæval art is charming, but mediæval emotions are out of date. One can use them in fiction, of course ; but then the only things that one can use in fiction are the only things that one has ceased to use in fact.

One should absorb the colour of life, but one should never remember its details. Details are always vulgar.

If one doesn't talk about a thing it has never happened. It is expression that gives reality to things.

Good resolutions are useless attempts to interfere with scientific laws. Their origin is pure vanity. Their result is absolutely nil. They give us now and then some of those luxurious, sterile emotions that have a certain charm for the weak. That is all that can be said for them. They are simply cheques that men draw on a bank where they have no account.

Each time that one loves is the only time that one has ever loved. Difference of object does not alter singleness of passion. It merely intensifies it.

Conscience makes egotists of us all.

We can have in life but one great experience at best and the secret of life is to reproduce that experience as often as possible.

Never trust a woman who wears mauve, whatever her age may be, or a woman over thirty-five who is fond of pink ribbons. It always means that they have a history.

Anybody can be good in the country. There are no temptations there. That is the reason why people who live out of town are so absolutely uncivilised. Civilisation is not by any means an easy thing to attain to. There are only two ways by which man can reach it. One is by being cultured, the other by being corrupt. Country people have no opportunity of being either, so they stagnate.

What nonsense people talk about happy marriages. A man can be happy with any woman so long as he does not love her.

The things one feels absolutely certain about are never true. That is the fatality of faith and the lesson of romance.

In the common world of fact, the wicked are not punished nor the good rewarded. Success is given to the strong, failure thrust upon the weak.

Modern morality consists in accepting the standard of one's age. I consider that for any man of culture to accept the standard of his age is a form of the grossest immorality.

The canons of Society are, or should be, the same as the canons of art. Form is absolutely essential to it. It should have the dignity of a ceremony as well as its unreality, and should combine the insincere character of a romantic play with the wit and beauty that make such plays delightful to us.

Sin is a thing that writes itself across a man's face. It cannot be concealed. People talk sometimes of secret vices. There are no such things.

No civilised man ever regrets a pleasure, and no uncivilised man ever knows what a pleasure is.

As for a spoiled life, no life is spoiled but one whose growth is arrested. If you want to mar a nature you have merely to reform it.

Most people become bankrupt through having invested too heavily in the prose of life. To have ruined oneself over its poetry is an honour.

Now-a-days all the married men live like bachelors and all the bachelors like married men.

Ordinary women never appeal to one's imagination. They are limited to their century. No glamour ever transfigures them. One knows their minds as easily as one knows their bonnets. There is no mystery in any of them. They ride in the park in the morning and chatter at tea parties in the afternoon. They have their stereotyped smile and their fashionable mauve.

Is insincerity such a terrible thing ? I think not. It is merely a method by which we can multiply our personalities.

The tragedy of old age is not that one is old, but that one is young.

Being adored is a nuisance. Women treat us just as humanity treats its gods. They worship us, and are always bothering us to do something for them.

The longer I live the more keenly I feel that whatever was good enough for our fathers is not good enough for us. In art, as in politics, 'les grand pères ont toujours tort.'

No woman is a genius. Women are a decorative sex. They never have anything to say—but they say it charmingly.

Humanity takes itself too seriously. It is the world's original sin. If the cave men had known how to laugh history would have been different.

I wonder who it was defined man as a rational animal. It was the most premature definition ever given. Man is many things, but he is not rational.

The people who have adored me have always insisted on living on long after I had ceased to care for them or they to care for me. They have become stout and tedious, and when I meet them they go in at once for reminiscences. That awful memory of woman ! What a fearful thing it is ! And what an utter intellectual stagnation it reveals !

Examinations are pure humbug from beginning to end. If a man is a gentleman he knows quite enough, and if he is not a gentleman whatever he knows is bad for him.

As for believing things, I can believe anything provided that it is quite incredible.

Credit is the capital of a younger son, and he can live charmingly on it.

There are only two kinds of women—the plain and the coloured. The plain women are very useful. If you want to gain a reputation for respectability you have merely to take them down to supper. The other women are very charming. They commit one mistake, however—they paint in order to try and look young.

The way of paradoxes is the way of truth. To test reality we must see it on the tight-rope. When the verities become acrobats we can judge them.

Beauty is a form of genius—is higher, indeed, than genius, as it needs no explanation. It is one of the great facts of the world, like sunlight, or springtime, or the reflection in dark water of that silver shell we call the moon. To me beauty is the wonder of wonders. It is only shallow people who do not judge by appearances. The true mystery of the world is the visible, not the invisible.

There are many things that we would throw away if we were not afraid that others might pick them up.

What a fuss people make about fidelity. Why, even in love it is purely a question for physiology. It has nothing to do with our own will : young men want to be faithful and are not, old men want to be faithless and cannot—that is all one can say.

Nothing can cure the soul but the senses, just as nothing can cure the senses but the soul.

I can stand brute force, but brute reason is quite unbearable. There is something unfair about its use. It is hitting below the intellect.

An artist should create beautiful things, but should put nothing of his own life into them. We live in an age when men treat art as if it were meant to be a form of autobiography. We have lost the abstract sense of beauty.

The thoroughly well-informed man is

the modern ideal. And the mind of the thoroughly well-informed man is a dreadful
thing. It is like a bric-a-brac shop, all monsters and dust, with everything priced above
its proper value.

Those who are faithful know only the
trivial side of love ; it is the faithless who
know love's tragedies.

A man cannot be too careful in the choice
of his enemies. I have not got one who is a
fool. They are all men of some intellectual
power, and consequently they all appreciate
me.

I like persons better than principles, and
I like persons with no principles better than
anything else in the world.

Women have no appreciation of good
looks in men—at least good women have
none.

The aim of life is self-development. To
realise one's nature perfectly—that is what
each of us is here for.

The ugly and the stupid have the best of

it in this world. They can sit at their ease and gape at the play. If they know nothing of victory they are at least spared the knowledge of defeat.

There is no such thing as a good influence. All influence is immoral from the scientific point of view.

Secrecy seems to be the one thing that can make modern life mysterious or marvellous to us. The commonest thing is delightful if one only hides it.

The only way to get rid of a temptation is to yield to it. Resist it and your soul grows sick with longing for the things it has forbidden to itself.

There is a fatality about all physical and intellectual distinction. It is better not to be different from one's fellows.

How fond women are of doing dangerous things. It is one of the qualities in them that I admire most. A woman will flirt with anybody in the world as long as other people are looking on.

It is perfectly monstrous the way people go about now-a-days saying things against one behind one's back that are absolutely and entirely true.

The one charm of the past is that it is the past. But women never know when the curtain has fallen. They always want a sixth act, and as soon as the interest of the play is entirely over they propose to continue it. If they were allowed their way every comedy would have a tragic ending and every tragedy would culminate in a farce. They are charmingly artificial, but they have no sense of art.

The real tragedy of the poor is that they can afford nothing but self-denial. Beautiful sins, like beautiful things, are the privilege of the rich.

With an evening coat and a white tie anybody—even a stockbroker—can gain a reputation for being civilised.

Never marry a woman with straw-coloured hair. They are so sentimental.

It is the very passions about whose origin we deceive ourselves that tyrannise most strongly over us. Our weakest motives are those of whose nature we are conscious.

It often happens that when we think we are experimenting on others we are really experimenting on ourselves.

The only difference between a caprice and a lifelong passion is that the caprice lasts a little longer.

People say sometimes that beauty is only superficial. That may be so, but at least it is not so superficial as thought is.

It is only the intellectually lost who ever argue.

Now-a-days most people die of a sort of creeping common-sense, and discover when it is too late that the only things one never regrets are one's mistakes.

Lady Henry Wotton was a curious woman, who was usually in love with somebody, and, as her passion was never returned, had kept all her illusions. She tried to look picturesque but only succeeded in being untidy, and her dresses always looked as if they had been designed in a rage and put on in a tempest.

Whenever a man does a thoroughly stupid thing it is always from the noblest motives.

To get back one's youth one has merely to repeat one's follies.

The reason we all like to think so well of others is that we are all afraid for ourselves. The basis of optimism is sheer terror. We think that we are generous because we credit our neighbours with the possession of those virtues that are likely to be a benefit to us. We praise the banker that we may overdraw our account, and find good qualities in the highwayman in the hope that he may spare our pockets.

I never take any notice of what common people say, and I never interfere with what charming people do.

Experience is of no ethical value. It is merely the name men give to their mistakes.

Moralists have, as a rule, regarded it as a mode of warning, have claimed for it a certain ethical efficacy in the formation of character, have praised it as something that teaches us what to follow and shows us what to avoid. But there is no motive power in experience. It is as little of an active cause as conscience itself. All that it really demonstrates is that our future will be the same as our past and that the sin we have done once, and with loathing, we shall do many times, and with joy.

Laughter is not at all a bad beginning for a friendship, and it is by far the best ending for one.

I choose my friends for their good looks, my acquaintances for their good characters, and my enemies for their good intellects.

I like Wagner's music better than anybody's. It is so loud that one can talk the whole time without other people hearing what one says.

You don't know what an existence they lead down there. It is pure, unadulterated country life. They get up early because they have so much to do, and go to bed early because they have so little to think about.

If one puts forward an idea to an Englishman—which is always a rash thing to do—he never dreams of considering whether the idea is right or wrong. The only thing he considers of any importance is whether one believes it oneself. The value of an idea has nothing whatever to do with the sincerity of the man who expresses it. Indeed, the more insincere the man is, the more purely intellectual will the idea be, and in that case it will not be coloured by wither his wants, his desires or his prejudices.

All art is quite useless.

THE CRITIC AS ARTIST

T HERE IS one thing worse than
In justice, and that is Justice without
her sword in her hand. When Right is not
Might, it is Evil.

Society often forgives the criminal. It
never forgives the dreamer.

It is always with the best intentions that
the worst work is done.

As long as war is regarded as wicked it
will always have a fascination. When it is
looked upon as vulgar it will cease to be popular.

To know the principles of the highest art
is to know the principles of all the arts.

Self-culture is the true ideal for man.
The development of the race depends on the
development of the individual, and where

self-culture has ceased to be the ideal the intellectual standard is instantly lowered and often ultimately lost.

Emotion for the sake of emotion is the aim of art, and emotion for the sake of action is the aim of life and of that practical organisation of life that we call society.

To be natural is to be obvious, and to be obvious is to be inartistic.

One is tempted to define man as a rational animal who always loses his temper when he is called upon to act in accordance with the dictates of reason.

Conversation should touch everything, but should concentrate itself on nothing.

The essence of thought, as the essence of life, is growth.

We are never more true to ourselves than when we are inconsistent.

Music creates for one a past of which one has been ignorant, and fills one with a sense of sorrows that have been hidden from one's tears. I can fancy a man who has led a perfectly common-place life, hearing by chance some curious piece of music, and suddenly discovering that his soul, without his being conscious of it, had passed through terrible experiences, and known fearful joys, or wild romantic loves, or great renunciations.

The public is wonderfully tolerant ; it forgives everything except genius.

What is truth ? In matters of religion it is simply the opinion that has survived. In matters of science it is the ultimate sensation. In matters of art it is one's last mood.

A little sincerity is a dangerous thing, and a great deal of it is absolutely fatal.

Life cheats us with shadows, like a puppet-master. We ask it for pleasure. It gives it to us, with bitterness and disappointment in its train. We come across some noble grief that we think will lend the purple dignity of tragedy to our days, but it passes away from us, and things less noble take its place, and on some grey, windy dawn, or odorous eve of silence and of silver, we find ourselves looking with callous wonder, or dull heart of stone, at the tress of gold-flecked hair that we had once so wildly wor-shipped and so madly kissed.

There are two ways of disliking art. One is to dislike it and the other to like it ratio-nally.

The sure way of knowing nothing about life is to make oneself useful.

An idea that is not dangerous is unwor-thy of being called an idea at all.

The one duty we owe to history is to re-write it.

The meaning of any beautiful created thing is at least as much in the soul of him who looks at it, as it was in his soul who wrought it. Nay, it is rather the beholder who lends to the beautiful thing its myriad meanings, and makes it marvellous for us, and sets it in some new relation to the age, so that it becomes a vital portion of our lives and a symbol of what we pray for, or perhaps of what, having prayed for, we fear that we may receive.

To do nothing at all is the most difficult thing in the world, the most difficult and the most intellectual. To Plato, with his passion for wisdom, this was the noblest form of energy. To Aristotle, with his passion for knowledge, this was the noblest form of energy also. It was to this that the passion for holiness led the saint and the mystic of mediæval days.

Learned conversation is either the affectation of the ignorant or the profession of the mentally unemployed.

Education is an admirable thing, but it is well to remember from time to time that nothing that is worth knowing can be taught.

Mediocrity weighing mediocrity in the balance, and incompetence applauding its brother—that is the spectacle which the artistic activity of England affords us from time to time.

When a man acts he is a puppet. When he describes he is a poet.

Life ! Life ! Don't let us go to life for our fulfilment or our experience. It is a thing narrowed by circumstances, incoherent in its utterance, and without that fine correspondence of form and spirit which is the only thing that can satisfy the artistic and critical temperament. It makes us pay too high a price for its wares, and we purchase the meanest of its secrets at a cost that is monstrous and infinite.

What we want in artists are unpractical people who see beyond the moment, and think beyond the day.

One tires, at the end, of the work of individuals whose individuality is always noisy, and generally uninteresting.

People sometimes say that fiction is getting too morbid. As far as psychology is concerned it has never been morbid enough.

We teach people how to remember : we never teach them how to grow.

While, in the opinion of society, contemplation is the gravest thing of which any citizen can be guilty, in the opinion of the highest culture it is the proper occupation of man.

Life is terribly deficient in form. Its catastrophes happen in the wrong way and to the wrong people. There is a grotesque horror about its comedies, and its tragedies seem to culminate in farce. One is always wounded when one approaches it. Things last either too long or not long enough.

Beauty has as many meanings as man has moods. It is the symbol of symbols. It reveals everything, because it expresses nothing. When it shows us itself it shows us the whole fiery-coloured world.

Anything approaching to the free play of the mind is practically unknown amongst us. People cry out against the sinner, yet is is not the sinful but the stupid who are our shame. There is no sin except stupidity.

It is through art, and through art only,

that we can realise our perfection ; through art, and through art only, that we can shield ourselves from the sordid perils of actual existence.

It is so easy to convert others. It is so difficult to convert oneself.

It is sometimes said that the tragedy of an artist's life is that he cannot realise his ideal. But the true tragedy that dogs the steps of most artists is that they realise their ideal too absolutely. For when the ideal is realised, it is robbed of its wonder and its mystery, and becomes simply a new starting-point for an ideal that is other than itself.

People who go in for being consistent have just as many moods as others have. The only difference is that their moods are rather meaningless.

All art is immoral, and all thought is dangerous.

Just as it is only by contact with the art of foreign nations that the art of a country gains that individual and separate life that we call nationality, so, by curious inversion, it is only by intensifying his own personality that the critic can interpret the personality of others ; and the more strongly this personality enters into the interpretation the more real the interpretation becomes—the more satisfying, the more convincing, and the more true.

The man who regards his past is a man who deserves to have no future to look forward to.

He to whom the present is the only thing that is present knows nothing of the age in which he lives. To realise one's own century one must realise every century that has preceded it and that has contributed to its making.

Those who try to lead the people can only do so by following the mob. It is through the voice of one crying in the wilderness that the way of the gods must be prepared.

It is very much more difficult to talk

about a thing than to do it. In the sphere of actual life that is, of course, obvious. Anybody can make history; only a great man can write it.

What is the difference between literature and journalism ? Journalism is unreadable and literature is unread.

Self-denial is simply a method by which man arrests his progress, and self-sacrifice a survival of the mutilation of the savage, part of that old worship of pain which is so terrible a factor in the history of the world, and which even now makes its victims day by day and has its altars in the land.

What is termed sin is an essential element of progress. Without it the world would stagnate or grow old or become colourless. By its curiosity it increases the experience of the race. Through its intensified assertion of individualism it saves us from the commonplace. In its rejection of the current notions about morality it is one with the higher ethics.

The longer one studies life and literature the more strongly one feels that behind everything that is wonderful stands the individual, and that it is not the moment that makes the man but the man who creates the age.

It is difficult not to be unjust to what one loves.

Formerly we used to canonise our heroes. The modern method is to vulgarise them. Cheap editions of great books may be delightful, but cheap editions of great men are absolutely detestable. Every great man now-a-days has his disciples ; and it is invariably Judas who writes the biography.

Words have not merely music as sweet as that of viol and lute, colour as rich and vivid as any that makes lovely for us the canvas of the Venetian or the Spaniard, and plastic form no less sure and certain than that which reveals itself in marble or in bronze, but thought and passion and spirituality are theirs also—are theirs, indeed, alone.

When people talk to us about others they are usually dull. When they talk to us about themselves they are nearly always interesting, and if one could shut them up when they become wearisome as easily as one can shut up a book of which one has grown wearied they would be perfect absolutely.

To have a capacity for a passion, and not to realise it is to make oneself incomplete and limited.

For those who are not artists, and to whom there is no mode of life but the actual life of fact, pain is the only door to perfection.

Humanity will always love Rousseau for having confessed his sins, not to a friend, but to the world.

The chief thing that makes life a failure from the artistic point of view is that thing which lends to life its sordid security—the fact that one can never repeat exactly the same emotion.

Modern pictures are, no doubt, delightful to look at. At least, some of them are. But they are quite impossible to live with ; they are too clever, too assertive, too intellectual. Their meaning is too obvious and their method too clearly defined. One exhausts what they have to say in a very short time, and then they become as tedious as one's relations.

It is so easy for people to have sympathy with suffering. It is so difficult for them to have sympathy with thought.

There is nothing sane about the worship of beauty. It is too splendid to be sane. Those of whose lives it forms the dominant note will always seem to the world to be mere visionaries.

Man is least himself when he talks in his own person. Give him a mask and he will tell you the truth.

The English public always feels perfectly at its ease when a mediocrity is talking to it.

In every sphere of life form is the beginning of things. Forms are the food of faith,

cried Newman, in one of those great moments of sincerity that make us admire and
know the man. He was right, though he
may not have known how terribly right he
was. The Creeds are believed not because
they are rational but because they are re-
peated. Yes ; form is everything. It is the
secret of life. Find expression for a sorrow
and it will become dear to you. Find expression for a joy and you intensify its ec-
stasy. Do you wish to love ? Use love's
litany and the words will create the yearn-
ing from which the world fancies that they
spring. Have you a grief that corrodes your
heart ? Learn its utterance from Prince
Hamlet and you will find that mere expression is a mode of consolation and that
form, which is the birth of passion, is also
the death of pain. And so to return to the
sphere of art, it is form that creates not
merely the critical temperament but also
the æsthetic instinct that reveals to one all
things under the condition of beauty. Start
with the worship of form and there is no secret in art that will not be revealed to you.

Modern memoirs are generally written by people who have entirely lost their memories and have never done anything worth recording.

Some resemblance the creative work of the critic will have to the work that has stirred him to creation, but it will be such resemblance as exists, not between nature and the mirror that the painter of landscape or figure may be supposed to hold up to her, but between nature and the work of the decorative artist. Just as on the flowerless carpets of Persia tulip and rose blossom indeed, and are lovely to look on, though they are not reproduced in visible shape or line so the critic reproduces the work that he criticises in a mode that is never imitative, and part of whose charm may really consist in the rejection of resemblance, and shows us in this way not merely the meaning but also the mystery of beauty, and by transforming each art into literature solves once for all the problem of art's unity.

THE DECAY OF LYING

❦

THINKING is the most un-
healthy thing in the world, and people die of it just as they die of any other
disease.

One touch of Nature may make the
whole world akin, but two touches of Nature will destroy any work of Art.

Art itself is really a form of exaggeration ; and selection, which is the very spirit
of Art, is nothing more than an intensified
mode of over emphasis.

No real artist ever sees things as they really are.

It is only the modern that ever becomes
old-fashioned.

Art creates an incomparable and un-
ique effect, and having done so passes on to

other things. Nature, on the other hand, forgetting that imitation can be made the sincerest form of insult, keeps on repeating the effect until we all become absolutely wearied of it.

The popular cry of our time is : Let us return to Life and Nature, they will recreate Art for us and send the red blood coursing through her veins ; they will shoe her feet with swiftness and make her hand strong. But, alas ! we are mistaken in our amiable and well-meant efforts. Nature is always behind the age. And as for Life, she is the solvent that breaks up Art, the enemy that lays waste her house.

The spirit of an age may be best expressed in the abstract ideal arts, for the spirit itself is abstract and ideal.

Many a young man starts in life with a natural gift for exaggeration which, if nurtured in congenial and sympathetic surroundings, or by the imitation of the best models, might grow into something really great and wonderful. But, as a rule, he comes to nothing. He either falls into care-less habits of accuracy or takes to frequent-ing the society of the aged and the well-in-formed. Both things are equally fatal to his imagination.

All bad art comes from returning to Life and Nature, and elevating them into ideals. Life and Nature may sometimes be used as part of Art's rough material, but before they are of any real service to Art they must be translated into artistic conventions. The moment Art surrenders its imaginative medium it surrenders everything. As a method Realism is a complete failure, and the two things that every artist should avoid are modernity of form and modernity of subject-matter.

Nothing is so fatal to a personality as the keeping of promises, unless it be telling the truth.

As long as a thing is useful or necessary to us or affects us in any way, either for pain or pleasure, or appeals strongly to our sym-pathies or is a vital part of the environment in which we live, it is outside the proper sphere of Art.

Literature always anticipates Life. It does not copy it, but moulds it to its purpose.

Just as those who do not love Plato more than Truth cannot pass beyond the threshold of the Academe, so those who do not love Beauty more than Truth never know the inmost shrine of Art.

Perplexity and mistrust fan affection into passion, and so bring about those beautiful tragedies that alone make life worth living. Women once felt this, while men did not, and so women once ruled the world.

Man can believe the impossible, but man can never believe the improbable.

When Art is more varied Nature will, no doubt, be more varied also.

If a man is sufficiently imaginative to produce evidence in support of a lie he might just as well speak the truth at once.

The ancient historians gave us delightful

fiction in the form of fact ; the modern nov-
elist presents us with dull facts under the
guise of fiction.

Nature is no great mother who has borne
us. She is our own creation. It is in our
brain that she quickens to life. Things are
because we see them, and what we see and
how we see it depends on the arts that have
influenced us. To look at a thing is very
different from seeing a thing. One does not
see anything until one sees its beauty.

The proper school to learn Art in is not
Life but Art.

The more we study Art, the less we
care for Nature. What Art really reveals to
us is Nature's lack of design, her curious
cru-dities, her extraordinary monotony, her
absolutely unfinished condition. It is fortunate for us, however, that Nature is so
imperfect, as otherwise we should have had
no Art at all. Art is our spirited protest,
our gallant attempt to teach Nature her
proper place. As for the infinite variety of
Nature, that is a pure myth. It is not to be

found in Nature herself. It resides in the imagination or fancy or cultivated blindness of the man who looks at her.

The aim of the liar is simply to charm, to delight, to give pleasure. He is the very basis of civilised society.

Art begins with abstract decoration, with purely imaginative and pleasurable work dealing with what is unreal and nonexistent. This is the first stage. Then Life becomes fascinated with this new wonder, and asks to be admitted into the charmed circle. Art takes life as part of her rough material, recreates it and refashions it in fresh forms ; is absolutely indifferent to fact ; invents, imagines, dreams, and keeps between herself and reality the impenetrable barrier of beautiful style, of decorative or ideal treatment. The third stage is when Life gets the upper hand and drives Art out into the wilderness. This is the true decadence, and it is from this that we are now suffering.

Life holds the mirror up to art, and either

reproduces some strange type imagined by painter or sculptor or realises in fact what has been dreamed in fiction.

People seldom tell the truths that are worth telling. We ought to choose our truths as carefully as we choose our lies, and to select our virtues with as much thought as we bestow upon the selection of our enemies.

To lie finely is an art, to tell the truth is to act according to nature.

Art finds her own perfection within, and not outside of, herself. She is not to be judged by any external standard of resem-blance. She is a veil rather than a mirror. She has flowers that no forests know of, birds that no woodland possesses. She makes and unmakes many worlds, and can draw the moon from heaven with a scarlet thread. Hers are the 'forms more real than living man,' and hers the great archetypes, of which things that have existence are but unfinished copies. Nature has, in her eyes, no laws, no uniformity. She can work mir-acles at her will, and when she calls mon-

sters from the deep they come. She can bid
the almond-tree to blossom in winter and
send the snow upon the ripe cornfield. At
her word the frost lays its silver finger on
the burning mouth of June, and the winged
lions creep out from the hollows of the Ly-
dian hills. The dryads peer from the thick-
et as she passes by, and the brown fauns
smile strangely at her when she comes near
them. She has hawk-faced gods that worship her, and the centaurs gallop at her side.

PEN, PENCIL
AND POISON

❦

THE FACT of a man being a poison-
er is nothing against his prose. The
domestic virtues are not the true basis of art.

It is only the Philistine who seeks to
estimate a personality by the vulgar test of
production.

All beautiful things belong to the
same age.

It has often been made a subject of re-
proach against artists that they are lacking
in wholeness and completeness of nature.
As a rule this must necessarily be so. That
very concentration of vision which is the
characteristic of the artistic temperament is
in itself a mode of limitation. To those who
are preoccupied with the beauty of form
nothing else seems of so much importance.

THE TRUTH
OF MASKS

❧

THE TRUTHS of metaphysics are the Truths of Masks.

Better to take pleasure in a rose than to put its root under a microscope.

Costume is a growth, an evolution, and a most important, perhaps the most important, sign of the manners, customs, and mode of life of each century.

Of Shakespeare it may be said that he was the first to see the dramatic value of doublets and that a climax may depend on a crinoline.

In Art there is no such thing as a universal truth. A Truth in Art is that whose contradictory is also true.

THE PORTRAIT
OF MR W. H.

❧

A THING is not necessarily true because a man dies for it.

It is always a silly thing to give advice, but to give good advice is fatal.

Art is to a certain degree a mode of acting, an attempt to realise one's own personality on some imaginative plane out of the reach of the trammelling accidents and limitations of real life.

Freckles run in Scotch families just as gout does in English families.

We have no right to quarrel with an artist for the conditions under which he chooses to present his work.

LORD ARTHUR
SAVILE'S CRIME

❧

ROMANCE IS the privilege of the rich, not the profession of the unemployed, The poor should be practical and prosaic.

It is better to have a permanent income than to be fascinating.

The inordinate passion for pleasure is the secret of remaining young.

Surely Providence can resist temptation by this time.

Are we not better than chessmen, moved by an unseen power, vessels the potter fashions at his fancy, for honour or for shame.

Many men prefer the primrose path of alliance to the steep heights of duty.

If a woman cannot make her mistakes charming she is only a female.

True romance is not killed by reality.

Actors are so fortunate. They can choose whether they will appear in tragedy or in comedy, whether they will suffer or make merry, laugh or shed tears. But in real life it is different. Most men and women are forced to perform parts for which they have no qualifications. The world is a stage, but the play is badly cast.

Comfort is the only thing our civilisation can give us.

The proper basis for marriage is a mutual misunderstanding.

LECTURES
AND ESSAYS

❦

BEAUTY is the only thing that time cannot harm. Philosophies fall away like sand, creeds follow one another, but what is beautiful is a joy for all seasons, a possession for all eternity.

He who stands most remote from his age is he who mirrors it best.

Love art for its own sake and then all things that you need will be added to you. This devotion to beauty and to the creation of beautiful things is the test of all great civilisations ; it is what makes the life of each citizen a sacrament and not a speculation.

To know nothing about our great men is one of the necessary elements of English education.

To disagree with three-fourths of England on all points is one of the first elements of vanity, which is a deep source of consolation in all moments of spiritual doubt.

We spend our days, each one of us, in looking for the secret of life. Well, the secret of life is in art.

THE SOUL OF MAN
UNDER SOCIALISM

❦

DISOBEDIENCE, in the eyes of anyone who has read history, is man's original virtue. It is through disobedience that progress has been made—through disobedience and rebellion.

The only thing that one really knows about human nature is that it changes.

Anybody can sympathise with the sufferings of a friend, but it requires a very fine nature to sympathise with a friend's success.

Selfishness is not living as one wishes to live, it is asking others to live as one wishes to live : and unselfishness is letting other people's lives alone, not interfering with them.

A man who does not think for himself does not think at all.

All sympathy is fine, but sympathy with suffering is the least fine mode.

The true perfection of man lies, not in what man has, but in what man is.

There are three kinds of despots. There is the despot who tyrannises over the body. There is the despot who tyrannises over the soul. There is the despot who tyrannises over soul and body alike. The first is called the prince. The second is called the pope. The third is called the people.

It was a fatal day when the public discovered that the pen is mightier than the paving-stone and can be made as offensive as a brickbat.

To recommend thrift to the poor is both grotesque and insulting. It is like advising a man who is starving to eat less.

A map of the world that does not include Utopia is not worth even glancing at, for it leaves out the one country at which Humanity is always landing. And when Humanity lands there it looks out, and, seeing a better country, sets sail. Progress is the realisation of Utopias.

The majority of people spoil their lives by an unhealthy and exaggerated altruism.

The work of art is to dominate the spectator. The spectator is not to dominate the work of art.

A true artist takes no notice whatever of the public. The public are to him non-existent.

The past is of no importance. The present is of no importance. It is with the future that we have to deal. For the past is what men should not have been. The present is what men ought not to be. The future is what artists are.

The Renaissance was great because it sought to solve no social problem, and busied itself not about such things, but suffered the individual to develop freely, beautifully, and naturally, and so had great and individual artists and great and individual men.

Man is complete in himself.

The State is to make what is useful. The Individual is to make what is beautiful.

A community is infinitely more brutalised by the habitual employment of punishment than it is by the occasional occurrence of crime.

The systems that fail are those that rely on the permanency of human nature, and not on its growth and development.

There is no one type for man. There are as many perfections as there are imperfect men. And while to the claims of charity a man may yield and yet be free, to the claims of conformity no man may yield and remain free at all.

A practical scheme is either a scheme that is already in existence or a scheme that could be carried out under existing conditions.

All imitation in morals and in life is wrong.

It is through joy that the Individualism of the future will develop itself. Christ made no attempt to reconstruct society, and consequently the Individualism that He preached to man could be realised only through pain or in solitude.

There is only one class in the community that thinks more about money than the rich, and that is the poor. The poor can think of nothing else That is the misery of being poor.

To live is the rarest thing in the world. Most people exist—that is all.

Personality is a very mysterious thing. A man cannot always be estimated by what he does. He may keep the law, and yet be worthless. He may break the law, and yet be fine. He may be bad without ever doing anything bad. He may commit a sin against society, and yet realise through that sin his true perfection.

Nothing should be able to harm a man except himself. Nothing should be able to rob a man at all. What a man really has is what is in him. What is outside of him should be a matter of no importance.

Some years ago people went about the country saying that property has duties. It is perfectly true. Property not merely has duties, but has so many duties that its possession to any large extent is a bore. If property had simply pleasures we could stand it, but its duties make it unbearable.

'Know thyself' was written over the portal of the antique world. Over the portal of the new world 'Be thyself' shall be written. And the message of Christ to man was simply : 'Be thyself.' That is the secret of Christ.

When Jesus talks about the poor He simply means personalities, just as when He talks about the rich He simply means people who have not developed their personalities. An echo is often more beautiful than the voice it repeats. An eternal smile is much more wearisome than a perpetual frown. The one sweeps away all possibilities, the other suggests a thousand.

DE PROFUNDIS

❦

MORALITY did not help me. I was one of those who were made for exceptions, not for laws.

There is no room for Love and Hate in the same soul. They cannot live together in that fair cavern house. Love is fed by the imagination, by which we become wiser than we know, better than we feel, nobler than we are : by which we can see Life as a whole : by which, and by which alone, we can understand others in their real as in their ideal relations. Only what is fine, and finely conceived, can feed Love. But anything will feed Hate.

Love does not traffic in a marketplace, nor use a huckster's scales. Its joy, like the joy of the intellect, is to feel itself alive. The aim of Love is love, and no less.

Those who have much are often greedy. Those who have little always share.

To reject one's own experiences is to arrest one's own development. To deny one's own experiences is to put a lie into the lips of one's own life. It is no less than a denial of the Soul.

There is nothing more beautiful than to forget, except, perhaps, to be forgotten.

The world divides actions into three classes : good actions, bad actions that you may do, and bad actions that you may not do. If you stick to the good actions you are respected by the good. If you stick to the bad actions that you may do you are respected by the bad. But if you perform the bad actions that no one may do then the good and the bad set upon you and you are lost indeed.

All trials are trials for one's life, just as all sentences are sentences of death.

We call ourselves a utilitarian age, and we do not know the uses of any single thing. We have forgotten that water can cleanse, and fire purify, and that the Earth is mother to us all. As a consequence our art is of the moon and plays with shadows. I feel sure that in elemental forces there is purification, and I want to go back to them and live in their presence.

No one can possibly shut the doors against Love for ever. There is no prison in the world into which Love cannot force an entrance.

Do not be afraid of the past. The past, the present and the future are but one moment in the sight of God, in whose sight we should try to live. Time and space, succession and extension, are merely accidental conditions of Thought. The Imagination can transcend them, and move in a free sphere of ideal existences. Things are, in their essence, what we choose to make them.